Machine Le

Absolute Beginners

A Simple, Concise & Complete Introduction to

Supervised and Unsupervised Learning Algorithms

Table of Contents

Introduction

Congratulations on downloading *Machine Learning for Absolute Beginners: A Simple, Concise & Complete Introduction to Supervised and Unsupervised Learning Algorithms*, and thank you for doing so. In the real world, companies like Amazon and Facebook and even YouTube use machine learning techniques to manage their functions efficiently. They are companies that use face recognition, speech recognition, image classification exploit k-means, deep neural networks, hidden Markov, SVM, etc. There are very many advances in machine learning that are coming up in the real world, and the applications of both supervised and unsupervised learning are growing. To get to understand what they are, you will need to get deep down into the basics, getting this book will help you have the best fundamental knowledge about machine learning.

To achieve this, the following chapters will differentiate what Supervised and Unsupervised learning are, helping you to have a better background to understand how they are used in the real world. This means that you will have to understand the analysis methods that need to come to play when you are dealing with lots of data, which is commonly defined as Big Data. The growing number of data needs to be processed with intelligent systems to bring about better solutions of the problems we are facing.

There are plenty of books that are on this subject; we are happy to help you choose this one. Every effort has been made to ensure that it is full of as much useful information as possible, please enjoy!

Chapter 1: Machine Learning Algorithm types

There is a classification that falls in machine learning algorithms which are based on the algorithm outcomes. There are several algorithm types that exist. They are listed below:

- Unsupervised learning: this involves specific inputs.

- Supervised learning: in this algorithm, there is a generation of a function that relates the output with the input. In supervised learning, the learning bit is the cause of the classification problem. The learner needs to know the function by looking at some I/O samples to map a vector into some classes.

- Semi-supervised learning - it combines the labeled and non-labeled samples to come up with a classifier or a function.

- Learning to learn: the algorithm in this type has to learn that the algorithm finds and learns the structure and bias that is dependent on the experience that happened.

- Transduction: it is quite the same as supervised learning, although it is not explicit in creating a function. Instead, it goes about to try and come up with fresh outputs that are dependent on the inputs or outputs that are being trained, and also totally new inputs.

- Learning that reinforces: the algorithm learns a new policy on how it will react when a particular observation is introduced. The impact that the algorithm has is directly felt in the environment which provides the results that help the algorithm to learn.

When you look at the performance and computations of machine learning algorithms, it is what is called computational learning theory. The topic of ML is all about the algorithmic design that makes a computer aware of the environment, adapt to it and learn it. Learning does not need to occur under a conscious structure. It only needs analysis of statistics, the regular occurrence of items, identifying patterns and predicting the next steps. This is completely different from the way a person learns something. The best part about learning algorithms is that they can provide insight into environments that are difficult to learn in a different approach.

We are currently in a historic period in our history, where computing has shifted to the cloud, from mainframes and PCs. This is not that big of a milestone, compared to what is coming in the next few years. What is even more revolutionary, are the computation tools and methods that are boosting computing. Currently, it is possible to create a complex algorithm that can crunch data for just a couple of dollars an hour.

To understand the machine learning algorithm types, you can also look at the sources below.

http://www.datasciencecentral.com/profiles/blogs/types-of-machine-learning-algorithms-in-one-picture

Chapter 2: Supervised Learning Approach

When you look at classification problems, the objective is for an algorithm or a software to learn the already created classification system. One example of a classification is how a computer learns how to recognize digits. In a general perspective, classification learning is the best approach to problems that deduce it, even though it is easy to determine the classification. There are cases where you don't have to give each instance a pre-determined classification if the responsible agent works the classification by itself. The description we have looked into is an example of unsupervised learning.

On the other hand, supervised learning normally leaves the probability for inputs not defined. If the inputs are available, there is no need to have this model. But if there are some inputs missing, it is hard to confirm the outputs. In unsupervised learning, there are variables that are responsible for the observations. This means that the results or the observations are available at the chain's end.

Supervised learning, according to training decision trees and networks, is the most common technique used. The techniques listed above rely on the provided info that is gotten from the classifications that are pre-determined. When you get to neural networks, the network error is determined by the classification used. This then leads to adjustment of the network by minimizing. In decision trees, the attributes that provide the information that is used to solve puzzles in classifications are the ones that are used in clarification.

We shall dive into this later on in the book. We are going to focus on the importance of supervision for both examples. This enables them to thrive because of their pre-determined classification.

Inductive ML is a learning process that involves a set of rules that are collected from samples. An example is a training set. It involves a classifier that generalizes relatively new instances.

Let us look at a step by step process of supervise ML.

Step1: dataset collection

When collecting a dataset, it is common also to have experts who can suggest the fields and attributes that are important. If that is not possible, then the easiest way is the brute force technique. This involves taking account of all available information, with the assumption that all features are already isolated. This type of data collection is not suitable for the process of induction since it has lots of noise and features that are missing. This makes it need a more detailed pre-processing step that is cumbersome.

Step2: data processing and data prep

There are several methods that one can choose from to be able to handle any kind of data missing. There have been researches that have identified the advantages and disadvantages of this technique. Let's look at the instant selection. It is used to cope with learning infeasibility from large data sets. An optimization problem that is instance selection tries to mine quality as it minimizes the size of another sample. Data is reduced, and data mines are maintained through an algorithm to work efficiently when exposed to big data sets.

Step3: feature subset selection

We are going to look at something that should be clear by now. The target of an algorithm that is learning is to use given inputs to minimize errors. In the problem of classification, the training set, which is the inputs, are examples which are used by the agent to enable learning. For examples, if you were going to learn XOR or exclusive OR, but you were shown one true and one false combination, but not both true or false, you will most definitely learn that the answer is true, always. The same applies to ML algorithms which involve data over-fitting and instead of learning a general classification technique, it memorizes the training set. One thing about training sets is that they don't have correct input class.

If the algorithm has a powerful memory, then it can lead to problems even on special cases that do not align with the principles that are common. Overfitting is common in this instance making it hard to identify powerful algorithms that can easily learn functions that are complex to provide outputs that are general.

Chapter 3: Unsupervised Learning Approach

This is much harder than supervised learning. The main objective is to have a computer that learns how to do something that it identifies all on its own, without human intervention. There are two ways that unsupervised learning approaches this kind of learning.

First approach

This involves teaching the agent using some reward system for it to know that it has achieved the results desired. There are no explicit categorizations that exist with this approach. This training style fits well with the framework of the decision problem since the classification makes choices that take advantage of rewards and not to produce classification. The technique we have looked at comes up with agents that generalize the world, and these agents are rewarded for engaging in actions that are needful. Additionally, there is a learning approach that is reinforced in unsupervised learning. This makes the agent base their actions on rewards that occurred previously with the need of any new information, which affect the world.

If you look at it carefully, this is a pointless technique, because the algorithm will know the reward that is awaiting it, and the agent is familiar with any processing, since it is familiar with any kind of processing that is expected. It is a beneficial approach and when calculating all possibilities takes a lot of time. It is hard to learn using the trial and error approach. On a different scale, this learning style can be useful since it does not assume pre-discovered classification.

An example is the backgammon game which was defeated with computer programs that were able to learn using unsupervised learning. The programs became strong with time and outmatched the best players in chess by playing themselves several times. The principles that these programs discovered perplexed the backgammon experts. The most interesting bit is that the programs even outdid backgammon programs that were trained using examples that were pre-classified.

Clustering is another level of unsupervised learning. In this learning method, a utility function is not going to be maximized on, but it has a goal of simply finding similarities in the data that is being trained. There is an assumption that exists about the clusters matching well with the classification that is intuitive. As an example, when you cluster individuals based on demographics, you might end up classifying the wealthy, on one corner, and the poor on the other corner. Since the algorithm will not use a name for assigning the clusters, there might be a production of the names, which will then be used to assign new examples into one cluster. When data is sufficient, a data driven approach can function better. For example, filtering algorithms that are used in social information like the ones used in Amazom.com, that are used to recommend books to site visitors. These algorithms use locating principles to get similar sets, then assigning new users to them. In some instances, like in information social filtering, the cluster information on members, can produce results that are meaningful. In some cases, the clusters can be a tool used by an expert analyst. It is sad to say that unsupervised learning suffers from overfitting training data.

Unsupervised learning algorithms are made to get structure from samples of data. The structures' quality is identified by the function of the cost that infers parameters that are optimal, through minimization. These parameters characterize the structure of hidden data. The same data structures need to be provided by a second set of the source data that has been used. When there is lack of robustness, overfitting becomes the noun, from the ML literature and the statistics.

Robust learning algorithms in sample fluctuations are derived from an array of results that are deviated, and also from the learning processing max entropy principle. Unsupervised learning can be called a champion in many fields; this is testament to the world backgammon program and in driverless cars. It can develop to become more advanced when there is a discovery of a new way to assign actions and values. When there is sufficient data, clustering comes on board, especially when there is additional data about specific cluster members, who are dependent on some data. It can also become tough at times. If the classifications are correct, classification learning becomes even more powerful. An example is the study of diseases. It is easy to come out from an autopsy, with the design of the disease; we can also have it easy when the classification is on the arbitrary thing that the computer can easily identify for us.

If we depend on the output of an algorithm as an input to some other system, then classification learning is important to that algorithm. Otherwise, it will be hard for anyone who wants to figure out the input means. As we have seen, both techniques are important and when you are choosing, figure out the circumstances of your choice. Identify the type of problem you are trying to solve, the time it needs for you to

solve it, and if supervised learning is possible.

Chapter 4: Algorithm types in Supervised learning

This area is concerned mostly with classification, and there are different algorithm types that are present here. These types include:

- Linear classifiers

-Perceptron

-Naive Bayes Classifier

-Logical Regression

-Support Vector Machine

-Bayesian Networks

-Neural Networks

-K-Means Clustering

-Quadratic Classifiers

-Decision Tree which includes Random Forests

-Boosting

Let's dive deeper into these algorithm types.

Linear Classifiers

The classification goal in ML is grouping similar times in groups. These items will have the same attributes and values. It has been stated that a linear classifier uses values of a linear combination of features to make the classification decision.

If there exists a 2-classification problem, a linear classifier can be visualized operating when it is split using a hyperplane, and a high dimensional input space. When this happens, on one side resides all points of the hyperplane which is "yes", while "no" is for the rest. When there is an issue on the speed of classification, then a linear classifier is often used. This is because it is way faster. As much as this is the case, a decision tree is also faster. When the number of dimensions is large, the linear classifier also thrives in this situation. This can be seen in document classification, where the number of counts in it represents each element. This calls for regularization of each classifier.

- Support Vector machine

An SVM constructs an N-type dimensional hyper balance to perform classification. This hyper plane separates data into 2 categories, optimally. They are neural network related.   To put this into perspective, a perceptron neural network has similarities to an SVM model that is using a sigmoid function.

An SVM is also closely related to the classic neural network that is a multilayer perceptron. An SVM is an option of a training method for multilayer perceptron, radial basis function, and polynomial classifiers. This occurs where the network's weight is discovered by coming up with a solution for a quadratic problem that has linear constraints. This is better than to solve an unconstrained, non- convex minimization problem, which is common or standard in neural network training.

Now, an attribute identified as a predictor-variable is used in the SVM literature, alongside a feature which is an attribute that is transformed, that define hyper-planes. With this in mind, feature selection is used to select the best representation. A vector, which is a group of features that describe a case is also used in this case. The SVM's goal is to define an optimal hyper-plane that differentiates vector clusters in a way that on one side, there are cases that have a target-variable category, and on the other side, there are cases that have the alternate category. We also have support vectors that are close to the hyper plane.

2-dimensional Example

We are going to look at an example. Let us imagine that we have a classification and we will use data that is attributed by target-variable having 2 categories. Let us also imagine that 2 predictor variables are present having continuous values. If we use the predictor's value of 1 predictor to plot a graph on X-axis and on Y-axis, you are going to see cases separation. In SVM analysis, the goal is to discover a line that splits the cases alongside their targets. The number of possible lines is numerous; the only question that poses is, "which is the best line? And how is the optimal line defined?"

When you see a dashed line laid down on parallel to the separation line of separation, it marks the separation between the nearest vector to the dividing line. The margin is the distance that lies between the dashed lines. The points or vectors that limit the margin width are what we call the support vectors.

In SVM analysis, we are going to find the oriented line so that support vectors margin is maximized. If all the analysis of s was comprised of 2 category target variables that have cluster points and 2 predictor variables was divided using a straight line, this would make the world a better place. Sadly, this is just a wish, and SVM has to deal with the following:

A) at least 2 predictor variables

B) Split the vectors that have nonlinear curves

C) Sort out cases where there cannot be cluster separation

D) Handle classifications that have more than 2 categories.

We are going to look at 3 main ML techniques and list examples on how they perform. These techniques include:

Neural Network

K-Means Clustering

Self Organized Map

K-Means Clustering

K-Means clustering guidelines that are basic are uncomplicated. We begin by defining the cluster K numbers and then assume the clusters' center. At the starting center, we are going to use any random object. Alternatively, we can also have the first K objects that are in the sequence to be the initial center. Now, with the goal of convergence in mind, the K means algorithm is going to perform three steps that are defined below.

1) Center coordinate determination

2) Distance from the center to each object

3) Based on the minimum distance, groups are created about the object.

According to some researchers, the K-Means is an unsupervised learning algorithm that is simply used to come up with solution of the clustering problem. There is a simple and easy procedure that is followed to classify any given data in clusters. The goal of these steps is to come up with k centroids of each cluster. Since different location alters the result, each centroid should be placed in a very intelligent way. The best way to achieve this is to separate them and place them in distant places from each other.

Next, you will have to take different points that belong to a set of data and find the centroid that is near, that you can associate it with. When you have no vector pending, you will have achieved the first stage where grouping occurs.

After the first stage, it is time to re-calculate the k new centroids from the previous step to come up with the clusters' bay centers. After achieving these centroids, the same dataset vectors and the newest and closest centroid will have to be bound. This will create a loop that will make it possible for us to see changes in the location of the k centroids on a step by step basis until it is not possible to create more changes.

Finally, the objective function is minimized by the algorithm, and in particular the squared error function. The steps are as follows:

1. the k points are spaced out using the clustered objects. These points are a representation of the centroids of the initial group.

2. The group that is close to the centroid is assigned an object.

3. A recalculation of the K centroid positions takes place when all objects are assigned.

4. Steps 2 & 3 are repeated until there is no more movement of the centroids. This finally brings about separated objects that are in groups that the metric being minimized is calculated.

Although it is possible to prove that there can be termination of the procedure, the most optimal configuration is not normally found using the k means algorithm. The algorithm, by its nature, is like a child who can easily catch a cold when exposed to cold environments. This is because it is very sensitive to the cluster centers that are normally initially selected randomly. To reduce the effect we have described, the k means algorithms can be executed more than once. This is a simple algorithm that you will find in many problem domains. We shall see how it is the best solution to fuzzy featured vectors. Let us look at an example:

Let us imagine we have x samples of feature vectors s_1, s_2, $s3$..., s_n. Which are from the same class, and they are categorized in k compact clusters, k<x. Let p_i refer to the vector's mean that are in cluster i. If there is a good separation of clusters, a minimum distance classifier can be used in their separation. We now state that s is in cluster i if$||s-pi||$ is the least of all the k distances. To find the k means, follow the list:

- Initial guesses for the means s_1, s_2, s_3,..., s_n

- This is until one cannot find any more mean changes

- The estimated mean is used to create clusters of the samples

- For i to k from 1

- The mean of all samples replaces pi for cluster i

- End for

- End until

This is an easy step by step procedure which can be viewed as an algorithm that is intense in the partitioning of the x samples into k clusters to minimize the sum of the distances that have been squared, to the centers of the clusters. The weaknesses that it possesses include:

- The initial values of the means are depended on by the results produced, and suboptimal partitions are identified frequently. Different points of the start are the solution that is standard.

- The initialization way was not specified. One starting way is the random selection of k of samples.

- It is possible to find empty samples that are close to s_i, so that there is no update on s_i. This annoyance needs to be sorted in the implementation.

- The metric that is used to measure $||s-p_i||$ is depended on the results. The most common solution is the normalization of each variable through standard deviation, even though it is not a good way to go about it.

- The value of k is required for the results to be seen.

Since we never know the number of clusters that exist, it makes the last problem even tougher. Looking at the example, we have looked at above; when you apply the same algorithm to the same data, a 3-means clustering is produced. Does it mean that it is way better than 2-means clustering?

Sadly, there is no way in heaven or hell that you will find a solution that will find the number of clusters of a dataset. You can easily compare the results of the multiple executions that have occurred using different k classes, then select the best one relating to the criteria of choice.

Naive Bayes Classifier

This is a method of supervised learning as well as a method of statistical classification. This is a probabilistic model that allows for the capturing of uncertainty in the model in a manner that is principled, using the outcomes probabilities. Predictive problems and diagnostic issues can be solved by Naive Bayes classifiers (NBC). NBC was named after the famous Thomas Bayes who came up with the theorem. This algorithm provides learning algorithms that are practical. This classifier is used in the provision of understanding and evaluating several learning algorithms. Explicit probabilities are calculated to be used in the hypothesis. Its robustness is evident in the input data noise.

Naive Bayes Uses

- Bayesian Classification is a method of probabilistic learning. The classifier, Naive Bayes is one of the most well-used algorithms for the classification of text documents for learning.

- Naive Bayes is also well known in the filtering of spam emails. Spam emails are easily identified by the classifier of Naive Bayes. Apart from the modern mail clients who use the algorithm, one can also install a different filtering program. Email filters like DSPAM, Spam Bayes, ASSP and Bogofilterutilize Bayesian filtering technique and its functionality is at times placed in the software of the mail server.

- Recommender Systems that are Hybrid. Data mining and machine learning techniques are applied by recommender systems to filter information that is unseen. It can also determine if a resource can be preferred by a given user. When you combine a collaborative filtering technique with a Naive Bayes classifier, a hybrid approach that has unique switching can be achieved. When this approach was tested on different sets of data, it showed that the algorithm being tested was scalable and gave out better performance, compared to other algorithms. At the same time, it eliminates some problems that are recorded by recommender systems.

- There is an online application in the link below that has successfully modelled Naive Bayes. This application that is online is an example of a Supervised ML and computing that is affective. With the use of a training set examples that reflect nasty, nice and sentiments that are neutral, Ditto has been trained to identify each differently.

http://www.convo.co.uk/x02/

- Modelling of simple emotion takes a model that is dynamical and a classifier that is statistically based. Naive Bayes takes each word and pairs of words as features. The utterances of users are classified into nasty, neutral and nice classes with labels of -1, 0 and +1 respectively. The numerical output that is achieved takes a simple 1st order dynamical system that represents the simulation of a simulated state.

The Theory of Bayes

The reasoning of Bayes is used in making decision and statistical inferences that deal with the inference of probability. In order for it to predict events in the futures, it uses the knowledge of the past events.

Let us look at an example.

Predicting colors of bricks in a box

rec	Age	Salary	Students	Loan rating	Computer purchase
R1	Equal or less than 30	High	No	Fair	No
R2	Less than or equal to 30	High	No	Excellent	No
R3	31 to 40	High	No	Fair	Yes
R4	Larger than 40	Medium	No	Fair	Yes
R5	Larger than 40	Low	Yes	Fair	Yes
R6	Larger than 40	Low	Yes	Excellent	No

R7	31 to 40	Low	Yes	Excellent	Yes
R8	Less than and equal to 30	Medium	No	Fair	No
R9	Less than or equal to 30	Low	Yes	Fair	Yes
R10	Larger than 40	Medium	Yes	Fair	Yes
R11	Less than or equal to 30	Medium	Yes	Excellent	Yes
R12	31 to 40	Medium	No	Excellent	Yes
R13	31 to 40	High	Yes	Fair	Yes
R14	Larger than 40	Medium	No	Excellent	No

The Theorem of Bayes

$$P(h/D) = \frac{P(D/h)\ P(h)}{P(D)}$$

P(h) means probability that is prior to the h hypothesis

P(D) means probability that is prior to the data that is to be trained D

P(h/D) means given D finding h's Probability

P(D/h) means given h, you find probability of D

On the table above, we are going to apply the theorem

D:represents a customer who is 35 yrs. old having a $50,000 PA

H: is a hypothesis that a computer can be bought by our computer

P(h/d): Finding the probability of customer D purchasing our computer, when we know that his income and his age are correlating. (35 yrs. Old and $50,000)

P(h): finding the probability that a customer of any age (probability that is prior) purchases our computer

P(D/h): Finding the probability that a customer is 35 years old and has an income of $50,000, with an already purchasedcomputer (probability that is posterior)

P(D): Finding the probability that one of our customers is aged 30 and has an income of $50,000

Bayesian Network

They are also known as Belief networks and they are part of the graphical models that are probabilistic. These structures represent uncertain domain knowledge. Each node represents a variable that is random, as the edges between nodes represent dependencies that are probabilistic corresponding variables, which are random. These dependencies that are conditional in the graph are estimated by the use of computational and statistical methods. Therefore, BN's merge principles from probability theory, graph theory, statistics and computer science. Undirected edge GM's are known as Markov networks or Markov random fields. These networks offer a simple independence definition between 2 nodes that are distinct based on Markov Blanket concept. In fields like computer vision and statistical physics, Markov networks are particularly popular.

BN also corresponds to directed acyclic graph (DAG) which is another structure of a GM, that is popular in machine learning, artificial intelligence, and statistical societies. BNs are what we call understandable and mathematically rigorous. An effective combination and effective representation of a probability distribution that is joint (JPD), has to be enabled over random variables.

There are two sets that define a DAG; these are set of vertices or nodes and a set of edges that are directed. The random variables are represented by the nodes, while the direct dependence is represented by the edges, which are among variables drawn using arrows located between nodes. An edge that is node X_i to X_j represents a dependence statistically between variables that are corresponding. Therefore, the arrow represents that variable X_j's value is dependent on the X_i value. X_i node becomes a parent of X_j, and X_j is referred to as a child of X_i. The acyclic graph structure ensures that no node can be its dependence or ancestor. An ancestor is a group of nodes where the node can be identified by a path that is different. On the other hand, a descendant is a group of nodes, where nodes can be identified on a path that is direct starting from the node. You should know that as much as the arrows indicate causal direct connection between variables, the process of reasoning can work on BNs by information propagation in any sort of direction.

A statement that is simple and conditionally independent is reflected by BN. Each variable is autonomous of the nondescendants if you consider the state of the parents. This property is used to minimize the no. of Parameters that characterize the JPD of variable. This brings about an effective way to calculate the probabilities of the posterior. Looking at the structure of the DAG which is normally referred to as a qualitative part, that needs to identify the parameters that are quantitative of the model. The parameters are identified in such a way that is consistent with the property of Markovian, where the distribution of the conditional property located at each node is dependent on its parents. For random variables that are discrete, a table represents the conditional probability, that lists the local probability, that feasible values are taken by a child node.

Boosting

Boosting is one of the strongest ML methods in existence today. Two of the well-known boosting algorithms, which include AdaBoost and Bagging, combine the decisions of a number of classifiers. In supervised learning, AdaBoost has been successful, but it is faced with several problems.

A) When the features are extremely large, training becomes unmanageable.

B) An imbalance exists between the negative samples and the positive samples for multiclass classification problems.

We are going to look at a 2-stage process of AdaBoost learning to select effectively, the discriminative features. Instead of boosting to occur in the original feature space, where there is high dimensionality, there will be a generation of multiple feature subspaces that have a low dimensionality. In the first stage, each subspace carries boosting. In the second stage, there is a combination of the simple fusion method and trained classifiers. When you look at the results of data that is sourced from facial expression recognition, our algorithm opposed that it can reduce the cost of training, and achieve a high classification performance.

The success that boosting algorithms have in supervised learning has extended to semi-supervised learning. The future looks bright when you look at the possibilities that come with combining boosting algorithm and graphs. This is with the intention of extending AdaBoost to semi-supervised learning and improve its performance.

The Functions of Gradient Boosting

There are 3 elements that are in gradient boosting.

a)An optimizable loss function

b)The addition of weak learners by the use of for loss function minimization

c)Making of predictions using weak learners

The Loss Function

To select a loss function solely depends on the problem in question. It has to be differentiated, but the beauty of loss functions is that many of them are able to work. There is no need to create a new-boosting algorithm for a loss function that is needed or supported; you can actually define one. For instance, squared error can be used by regression while logarithmic loss can be used by classification.

One major gradient boosting benefit is that a boosting algorithm can use a framework that is general, where a loss function uses a network that is differentiated.

The Additive Model

The addition of trees is done one at a time, while trees that exist remain unchanged. To minimize the loss in the tree addition process, one needs to use the procedure of gradient descent. The minimization of sets of parameters is done traditionally using gradient descent. The parameters that are commonly minimized include neural network weights and regression equation coefficients. After the error is calculated, or the loss is calculated, there is an update of the weights with the goal of error minimization.

Sub-models of weaker learners, like decision trees, is used instead of parameters. After the loss calculation, the addition of trees has to be done on the model that is in charge of reducing the loss, for the procedure of gradient descent to be performed. Parameterizing of the tree is the process that makes this happen. Modification of the tree parameters follows and finally, the residual loss is reduced as a sign of things flowing correctly. The general term for this process is functional gradient descent. Another alternative name functions in gradient descent.

The new tree's output is added to the existing trees sequence output to improve the model's final output. Once the loss gets to a level that is acceptable, or it stops improving on datasets that validate externally, the addition and training of a specific number of trees is done.

Weak Learner

When you look at gradient boosting, decision trees are the weak learners. Regression trees that output real values for splits, allow the addition of model outputs and the correction of predicted residuals. The creation of trees is done greedily. Basing on Gini and minimization of loss purity, the best points of splitting are selected.

When you look at AdaBoost, decision trees that are short and had one split were used. These single splits are called decision stumps, and 4-8 levels can be used in large trees. Weak learners can be constrained in some ways, like max no.of splits, leaf nodes, or layers. This ensures that there is a constant weakness in the learners, even though they can be constructed greedily.

Gradient Boosting improvements

Training data sets can be overfitted quickly by the use of a gradient boosting. Regularization methods that come from different sections of the algorithm can benefit gradient boosting, by improving the algorithms performance by the reduction of overfitting.

There are 4 gradient boosting enhancements techniques we shall be looking at.

- Tree Constraints

- Learning that is penalized

- Shrinkage

- Sampling Randomly

Tree Constraints

Weak learners possess skills even though they are weak. Constraining trees can be done in several ways. The more the number of creations of constrained trees there are, the more the number of trees that will be needed in the model, and vice versa. If there are fewer trees that are constrained, very few trees will be needed.

Here is a list of some constraints that one can impose, during the creation of decision trees.

The depth of the tree: You can say that deeper trees can be called complex trees, and shorter trees are the ones which are preferred. To get better results means using levels 4-8.

No. of trees: overfitting can be very slow when one is adding more trees in the model. What is recommended is the addition of trees until there is no improvement which can be observed.

No. of observations on each split: a constraint at its minimum is imposed on the data to be trained at the node of training, before considering a split.

No.of leaves: just like depth, no.of leaves can constraint the tree's size, but not to a structure that is symmetrical when the use of other constants is used.

Minimum loss improvement: this constraint on any slit's improvement is added to the tree.

Learning that is penalized

There can be imposition on the tree's parameters by the additional constraints, in addition to the tree's structure. CART, which is a classic decision tree, is not used as a learner that is weak; instead, a regression tree that is modified is used. This regression tree has values that are numeric in the terminal nodes, which are commonly referred to as leaf nodes. The value indicated on tree leaves can also be referred to as leaves.

The weight value of the leaves of the tree can use regularization like L1 regularization and L2 regularization to regularize.

For more details about boosting, kindly look at the sources below:

Neural Network

Several regression tasks can be done by neural networks. Although, each network works to handle one. In many instances, the network provides a single variable output. But in state classification problems, there might be some outputs that can be produced. The stage of post processing will handle the mapping of outputs to output variables. When multiple output variables are defined in a single network, cross talk may suffer. This means that the neurons that are hidden are going through a tough time in learning, as 2 different functions are being attempted. To come up with a better way means to use output to train the different network, and then to come up with an ensemble to run them as a single unit. The neural methods we are going to focus on include:

- Multilayer Perceptrons

It is the most popular network that is currently being used. We have looked at it briefly in other sections. Each unit performs a biased weighted sum of inputs that is passed through a transfer function for an output production. The units are placed in a feed forward kind of topology. The input output model of the network is therefore simple to interpret, with the biases and the weights of the model. Any kind of complex functions in this network can be modelled. Some of the issues that are a priority in the Multilayer Perceptron include the layers with their units, and the hidden layers. The problem defines the number of I/Os, even though the types of inputs which are going to be used is not certain. However, as of now, we shall stick with the assumption that the selection of the number of input variables is already complete. The hidden units that will be used are not clear. To start on a good point, a hidden layer needs to be used, having half the number of the I/O units.

Multilayer Perceptrons Training

After selecting the layers, units identified in the layers, the biases and the networks weight, they all have to be set to minimize the network prediction errors. This is what the ***training algorithms*** is created to do. To automatically adjust the biases and the weights, for error to be minimized, you need to gather historical cases. The process we have seen above relates to that of the networks model that presents the data available for training. One needs to run all the cases of training through the network in order to determine the error of a configuration, as you compare the real output generated with desired output. An *error function* combines the differences to provide the network error.

Summed squared error which is used for problems in the regression are the most common types of the error function. They are used where the output unit's errors on individual cases are summed up, squared, and a cross entropy function is used.

In linear modeling, which is a kind of traditional modelling, using an algorithm, it is easy to determine the configuration model, to have a reduced error. A neural networks nonlinear modelling power cost is a factor that one can never be so sure about, when it comes to lowering the error, even if you can adjust the network.

Each N weights & the networks biases are considered as an N+! Network dimension error. By weight configuration, one can easily plot the error in a N+1 dimension, which forms the error-surface. The main objective of the training of the network involves getting the many-dimensional surface lowest point. In a sum-squared error functions linear model, the error surface is quadratic, meaning that the curve is smooth with one minimum. This makes to identify the minimum. Some useless features characterize the complex neural network and error surfaces. These features include a local minimum which is a lower level of the terrain, but still over the global minimum. Others include plateaus, flat plots, long ravines and saddle points.

The errors-global minimum surface is hard to determine analytically. Therefore, the neural networks training is important to explore the error surface. It starts from random weights and biases configuration, to the training algorithms which seek the global minimum incrementally. Ideally, when it comes to the creation of a move downhill, the error of the surface needs to be computed at its current position. But at a later point, the algorithm halts at a low point, which can represent the local minimum, which needs to be the global minimum.

Algorithm of back propagation

This is the best example of a training neural network algorithm. Conjugate gradient descent, which is a modern 2nd order algorithm, is faster when it comes to many problems, together with Levenberg-Marquardt. But when it comes to back propagation, it has advantages when some circumstances present themselves. This makes it the easiest algorithm anyone can comprehend.

When you look at backpropagation, the calculation of the errors gradient vector is done. This vector is an idea as it looks at the slope, starting at the current point. Therefore, this makes it decrease the error when we move along a "short" distance. As the moves slow when the bottom is near, a minimum will be realized. The hard part is defining the size of each step.

When the large steps are taken, it is easy to overstep solutions or provide a wrong outcome. Looking at an example of neural network training, we can have an algorithm that continues slowly along a narrow, steep, bouncing between sides. On the contrary, tiny steps will provide the right solution, but the number of iterations needed is very many. Far from theory, the slope is proportional to the step size for the algorithm to settle at the minimum, to a special constant which is identified as a *learning rate*. When going for the learning rate, the right setting is application dependent; it may vary in time, and it gets smaller as with progression of the algorithm.

When a momentum term is included, the algorithm is often modified. The move is done in a fixed direction, so that in case some progress is made in the right way, the algorithm improves, which makes it escape the local minimum, making it move over plateaus rapidly.

The algorithm goes through **epochs** iteratively. The training cases on each epoch are submitted to the network, and the actual outputs and target are compared, and an error calculation is done. This error alongside the error surface gradient adjusts the weights, and the whole procedure is repeated. The first configuration of the network is random, and when some epoch is complete, the training stops. Other cases that can make the training to stop include stopping of the error to improve, or in cases where it gets to a level that is acceptable. One can select which stopping condition can be used.

- Generalization and over-learning

The primary issues with this approach discussed earlier on does not belittle the focused error. This expected error that the network makes when there are identified cases will still be available. To summarize, the most appealing part of the network is the generalization of the new cases. The network is built to minimize training set error, and even if there are no perfect training sets that are large, it is not similar to error minimization that is on the surface of the error of the unknown model.

The problem of over-fitting and over-learning is an important manifestation of the distinction. A polynomial curve is the best way to show this concept, compared to neural networks, even though they share the same concept.

When you look at a polynomial, you are looking at an equation that has constant and variables. For instance, if we replace 'Y' with 'b' and 'x' with 'a', our equation would be as follows:

$b=2a+3$

$b=3x2+4a+1$

There are various shapes for polynomials that are different. They also have large numbers. When you have a data set, you may fit a polynomial curve if you want to have the data interpreted. Most of the time, the data is noisy; therefore, don't expect always to see a smooth curve or the line to go through each point. A high order polynomial is very flexible, making it possible to fit the data using a shape that is unrelated, but a low order polynomial cannot for exactly close to the points.

The same problem is shared in neural networks. A more complex function is modeled with a network with weight patterns. This makes it easy to over-fit. When you have a network that does not have lots of weights, it won't be able to create a model of the function that is present, powerfully. For instance, a network that does not have hidden layers models is a representation of a simple linear function. How will it be possible to choose the correct network complexity? A large network will get an error, but it may be tagged with an over-fitting instead of the right modelling.

The best solution is to track the progress against a data set that is independent; this is called a selection set. These cases are not used in back propagation since they are used to keep track of each algorithmic progress. Instead, it will be discovered that the networks initial performance on the selection sets, and the training is the same. Even though it may not be ideally the same, but the division cases between the sets is based. When the training is in progress, you will notice a drop on the error of the training, and with the training, it minimizes the error function that is true, and the error of selection also drops. In case the error of selection stops from declining, but rises, the network will be overfitting the data and training will stop. When the training process is in progress, and overfitting takes place, this is identified as over-learning. This now leads to a decrease in hidden layers that exist, because the network is more advanced to counter the problem in question. On the flip side, if there is a weak network, to model the underlying function, there won't be an occurrence of overlearning, and it won't matter if the selection errors or the training error drops to a level that is satisfactory.

Problems that are related to the correct network size to use and the local minima mean that a neural network involves the testing of the different network as each network is trained several times to avoid being cheated by each local maxima and to observe each performance. The selection error is the right guide to performance. If we assume that all else is equal, it is preferable to have a simple complex instead of a complex one. You can choose a smaller network instead of a large one with a slight selection error improvement.

This approach that has repeated trials has a problem. The problem is that the selection set is used to primarily select the model. This makes it part of the training process. This makes it compromise its reliability as a guide to the model's performance. When you go through various trials, you may be lucky enough to get a network that can perform well on the selection set. It is important to use a test set of data that will increase the reliability towards the model's performance at larger scale. The test data tests the final modelling in order to ensure that the outcome of the training and selection sets, are not fakes. To achieve this goal, only one use of the test data is recommended. In case this is used to alter and repeat the process of training, the data that is selected will be realized.

It is unfortunate to have divisions in multiple subsets, given that less data is normally provided than the desired amount for a subset. Resampling is the best way to counter this problem. One can conduct experiments using different data divisions into selection, training and test sets. Several ways to look the subsets are available. This includes cross validation, bootstrap, and the Monte-Carlo resampling. If design decisions are made, like the best neural network configuration to use, based on the experiments with different subset instances, there would be a more reliable result produced. That experiment can be used to help in the decision making on the type of network to use and train the networks with samples, from the beginning. This intends to do away with the bias of sampling. There can be a retaining of the networks that work well in the sampling process. When the ensemble results are looked into, there is a mitigation on the bias of the sample. Looking at the summary, after all the technical and ins and outs seen above, the network design has some of the following stages:

- First, choose an initial configuration, one that has a hidden layer with some units that are hidden which are half the sum of the I/O inputs.

- You can conduct some experiments iteratively with each configuration, using the best network. Each configuration needs a couple of experiments to counter the trickery in the discovery of a local minimum during training, and when a chance of resampling is made possible.

- If under learning happens in each experiment, this leads to the networking missing the performance level. You will then have to add to the hidden layer some neurons for a trial. If you discover that there is no change, add a hidden layer. If under learning happens in each experiment, this leads to the networking missing the performance level. You will then have to add to the layer that is hidden, some neurons for trial purposes. If there is no change, then add a hidden layer.

- When the over-learning occurs, try removing some layers and hidden units.

- Once you have determined the best networks configuration,
  resample and create new networks that have the same
  configuration.

Data Selection

The stages we have looked at assume that the training, test data, and
verification must be representative of the model in question. In Neural
modelling, the same idea of GIGO, Garbage in Garbage out also applies.
The worth of the model relies on the training data, therefore, if it is not
well represented, then it is compromised, rendering it useless. Let us
look at the problems that can make the training set useless.

Training data is normally historical. But when situations change, then the
past data is not relevant. It is important to make sure that all scenarios
that are possible are covered. For a neural network to work well, it can
only use present case. For instance, if you render employees who have

incomes of $100,000 in a year as a bad risk, then if you have training data with employees who earn less than $40,000, then you should not expect the network to make the right decision when it deals with the unseen cases. It is wrong to use extrapolation when you are dealing with models, the downside in avoiding this, is that you will have neural networks that make predictions that are poor.

Easy features are learned easily by a network. To expound on this point, we are going to look at a classic example where a project that was premised with the task of identifying tanks automatically was put in place. In this project, the network in context was exposed to a 100 picture images that were not tanks, and 100 more pictures of tanks. It then achieves a score of 100%. But when test data is applied, it does not do well. What is the reason for this? The pictures which have tanks are taken when it is a rainy, dark day, while the picture which doesn't have the tanks are taken on sunny days. The differences in light intensity are what the network learns to differentiate. For it to work, the network needs cases of training on all kinds of lighting conditions and weather where it is expected to work on. You should also add pictures that have all kind of angles, terrain, and even distance.

Unbalanced data sets. It is critical to have the types of proportion data types because a network normally minimizes an overall error. If you load a network with data set that includes 900 cases that are good and 10 cases that are bad, it will make its decision with a bias to the good cases, to reduce the error. If in real proportion there is a bad representation of both the good & the bad, then the networks decision will most likely be wrong. The best example for this is on disease prevention. Now, a network is fed with training data that is on a 9 to 10 split. Later on, there are patient diagnosis that is based on complaint of a particular problem, where the tendency for the disease is on a 50 to 50 basis. The network here will fail to identify the disease in some patients who are unhealthy, because of its cautious reaction. On the contrary, if it is trained on the data complaint and a routine basis, then the network may flag quite some alerts. In these scenarios, the data set may be customized to take into consideration data distribution. For instance, you could remove some numerous cases and replicate the less numerous ones. The best approach always has the same representation of cases that are different, and that can interpret the decision of the network.

Self Organizing Map

SOFM network is used on a different scale when you compare it to alternative networks. Since many kinds of networks work primarily for supervised learning, unsupervised learning works well with SOFM. In supervised learning, cases have both input variables that need to inference by the network, through a mapping to the associated outputs. But in unsupervised learning, there are only input variables that are contained in the training data set. It seems strange, right? What does the network use if it only has the inputs and no outputs? To answer this question like a guru, the answer is really simple, SOFM network is the answer. SOFM tries to learn the data structure.

The SOFM network learns how to recognize data clusters and relate the same classes to one another. The data that refines the network that can be understood by the user when looked at carefully. Data classes can be labelled as well as recognized, in order for the network to properly classify tasks. SOFM networks come in handy when building classifications considering that output classes which are available can be used immediately. An advantage exists, because class similarities can be brought about.

Novelty detection is the 2nd possible use of SOFM network, because, when they have a training data, they can easily learn how to recognize clusters in it and provide a response. If new data which is different from the previous cases comes fourth, the network will not be able to recognize it, and there will be novelty created.

There are 2 layers in an SOFM network. We have an input layer and also an output layer, which is known to be as a topological map layer. The output's layer units are set in space in 2 dimensions. In SOFM networks, an algorithm that is iterative is used; They start with the initial center that make up a random set, which are then changed by the algorithm to be cohesive with the clusters of training data. It compares with sub-sampling and K-means algorithm are one love, to assign SOM network centers. Indeed, the algorithm used in SOFM can be used to allocate the center of the network types. Far from that, there is another level of operation that the algorithm performs at. The network is also arranged by a training procedure that is iterative to have units representing centers that are closer in the input space, to be placed closer to the topological map. You can look at the topological layer of the network as a 2-dimensional grid that needs to be distorted and folded in the input space that is the N-dimensional, to preserve the original structure. To represent the N-dimensional space in 2 dimensions will lead to the loss of detail. However, if the technique can allow the user to visualize data, it can be worth the while, even though it can be hard to understand.

Some epochs are run by the iterative Kohonen algorithm. On each epoch, it executes every case that is used in training, to apply the algorithms as follows.

A number of epochs are run by the iterative Kohonen algorithm. On each epoch, it executes every training case and applies the algorithms as follows:

- The winning neuron which is at the input's case center to be selected

- The neuron that wins then adjusted to be the same as the input case which is a weighted sum of the training case and the old neuron center

A time decaying learning rate is used in the Algor UTN for a weighted sum to be performed to make sure that the changes are subtle when the passing of the epochs is complete. This is with the aim of having settled centers that are at a compromise, which represent cases that lead to neutron winning. If the concept of the neighborhood is added to the algorithm, then the topological ordering property is achieved. A group of neurons that surround the neuron that wins is what is called the neighborhood. It also decays over time, just like the rate of learning, for most neurons to be in the neighborhood. Later on, the neighborhood compromises only the neuron that wins. The changes of the neurons are applied to all members of the existing neighborhood and the winning neuron in Kohene algorithm.

Initially, large network areas are dragged heavily to the training cases; this is the effect of the update in the neighborhood. A crude topological ordering which is the same as cases activation clumps of neurons is developed by the network. This is done in a topological map. When the learning rate and the neighborhood are passed by the epochs, they both decrease, for finer distinctions in the map areas can be shown, which then results to neurons that are fine tuned. The following two distinct phases are conducted in training:

- A short phase that has a neighborhood and high learning rates

- Long phase that has close to zero neighborhoods and low learning rates

Once the data structure recognition is mastered by the network, it can be used to examine the data through visualization. Win frequencies can easily be checked to see if there is a formation of a unique cluster on the expected map. There is an execution of individual cases and an observation of the topological map with an intention of finding out if clusters can represent some meaning. This normally involves the use of the original application area to form a relationship between the clustered cases. When you look at the topological map, neurons are labelled for you to identify their meaning, once the identification of the clusters are done. Once the topological map is different, there can be new submissions to the network. If there is a class name labelling in the winning neuron, classification can be done. If this does not happen, then the network is rendered undecided.

SOFM are inspired by the brain's unknown properties. The brain is a large sheet of folded paper that has known topological properties, like the arm is next to the area that corresponds to the hands. SOFM is inspired by the brain's unknown properties. The brain is a large sheet of folded paper that has known topological properties like the arm is next to the area that corresponds to the hand.

Advantages and Disadvantages of SOM

Advantages of SOM

One of the best things about SOMs is that they are simple and easy to comprehend. If they are close enough, and there is connection between them, then they are similar. In case there is a disconnection between them, then they are different. Unlike N-land and Multi-dimensional scaling, they can easily be understood and used effectively.

They also work very well. They can easily classify data and evaluate the data to make sure that the quality of the calculation makes the map good as it highlights the strength of the similarities between objects.

Disadvantages of SOMs

One problem is that each SOM is different and they all find different similarities in sample vectors. Sample data is organized in SOMs for the final product samples to be similar.   For instance, if you have lots of purple shades, you won't find a large group of the color in the cluster, sometimes you will get two different clusters. Just by the example of colors, we can point out the similarities between the two groups by color, but in most groups, the similarities won't be this obvious.

Therefore, tons of maps will need to be developed to get one loop.

Another problem is getting the correct data. One needs to provide a value for each dimension of member samples to create a map. It is not possible to have this scenario at times, and this makes SOMs have missing data.

Finally, SOMs are normally expensive in computation. This is one major fault because the data dimensions increase, the visualization of the dimension reduction escalates to become a priority, but at the same time, the computation time increases.

Chapter 5: Comparison of Supervised and Unsupervised Learning

1. Supervised Learning

2. Unsupervised Learning

Its fundamentals are based on training data that is sampled from a data source with the right classification that is assigned. These techniques are used in MultiLayer Perceptron (MLP) models and feedforward. There are three distinct features of MLP, they include:

- Hidden layers of neurons that are separate from the I/O network layers that make the network to provide solutions to tough problems.

- There is a high connectivity in the networks interconnection level

- There is a differentiable nonlinearity in the neuronal activity

Learning through training and the features listed above provides solutions to supervised learning algorithm for error correction. This algorithm performs training to the network concerning I/O samples. It then looks for the difference between the calculated output & the desired output, and the neuron weights are adjusted dependent on the error signal's product, together with synaptic weight's out instance.

Having laid out this principle, there are two faces where error back propagation learning happens.

Pass Forward

There is an introduction of the input to the network which then goes forward, coming out on the final stage as an output, after going through each step of the network.

Pass Backward

The output presented to the neuron of the output is moved backward in the network. It then calculates each neuron's local gradient in each layer and lets the synaptic weight to change concerning the delta rule.

This computation now continues for each input recursively, starting with the forward pass, then the backward pass until the network converges. Supervised learning of an Artificial Neural Network is okay since it provides solutions to nonlinear and linear possible like plant control, classification, prediction, robotics, and forecasting.

Unsupervised Learning

In SONN (Self Organized Neural Networks), learning is out carried through unsupervised learning algorithms to find patterns that are hidden in input data that is unlabeled. In unsupervised learning, it is possible to organize learned data without a signal of error to counter check on the solution. It is advantageous for the unsupervised learning when it lacks direction, because it allows for patterns to be identified by the algorithm, when it looks back on patterns that were not considered previously. Some of the major features of SOM include:

1. A signal pattern that is incoming is transformed to 1 or 2-D maps, with a target of an adaptive transformation.

2. A feedforward structure that has a single computational layer is represented by the network. The neurons in this structure are arranged in columns and rows.

3. All signals of input are stored in context to each stage.

4. Sensitive pieces of information that were related, are dealt with neurons that relate and next to each other by the use of connections that are synaptic.

Neurons compete against each other in order to be active in the competitive layer and the computational layer. Therefore, the algorithm that is used for learning is referred to as a competitive algorithm. There are three phases that Unsupervised algorithm work in SOM, this includes:

Competition phase

When the network is presented with input pattern x, the synaptic weight in the inner product is computed, and the neurons find a discriminant function in the competitive layer that motivates competition in the neurons. Close to the input vector, is the vector of the synaptic weight.

Cooperative phase

The topological neighborhood's center is determined by the winning neuron. This is achieved via lateral interaction of the neurons. Over a given period, the topological neighborhood reduces its size.

Adaptive Phase

Singular values of the discriminant function are increased on both the neighborhood & the winning neurons. This is related to the synaptic weight adjustment and the input pattern.

When the patterns in charge of training are repeated, the vectors of the synaptic weight will follow the input pattern distribution due to the neighborhood updating and the Artificial Neural Network learning, unsupervised.

In the process of classification, both learning methods group students in different characteristics. For instance, students who score high academically are categorized in a group, in another group, you will find students from less privileged backgrounds, and you will also find average students in another class.

The two results being observed are in favor of unsupervised learning since the percentage of correctness is high if you compare it with the supervised algorithm. When you look at the differences, they are not oceans apart, but with an additional layer, the correctness of the supervised algorithm can be increased. If you compare the time it takes to build a network and compare it with KSOM, it is more. Other issues that were managed by back propagation algorithm include:

Local gradient descent

By adjusting the weights, the output error is minimized by the gradient descent. The weight error change can make the error to range, leading to less reduction. This is what we call local minima. Using randomly initialized weight vectors solved this problem and when each iteration

passed, the current pattern of error updates the weight vector.

Network size

Problems that exist in the network size in classification that is linear, the

layer that is hidden is not needed, but three classifications are needed

on the error basis and on the trail to confine them in one hidden layer.

The neuron selection in the layer that is hidden is another problem.

Stopping criteria

An Artificial Neural Network halts the training after it has learned the

data patterns. This is done after learning mean squared error calculation

is done. Sadly, the total error for the classification with four hidden

neurons is 0.28 which cannot go further than that. When a trial is done

to reduce the minimum, validation error increases.

Classification is an active decision-making task that is used in our academic example above. This classification might enable in allowing the students to be mentored and improve their academic performance by training and adequate attention. Additionally, it helps students to identify the lack they have on their domain and improve in that skill which benefits the students and the institution.

A classification network that is designed using some patterns is a learning observation. A new class can be assigned to a class that is existing. New knowledge and theories are facilitated by this classification in input patterns. The neural network's learning behaviors enhance the properties of the classification. We have found that algorithms used in Supervised learning, which have error back propagation are efficient for quite a number of non-linear problems that occur in real time. This can be seen in the context of the classification of students we saw. In this scenario, the unsupervised model performs efficiently when you compare it to algorithms in supervised learning.

Summary

We would like to recommend you to look at the ebook *Machine Learning for Beginners: The Definitive Guide to Neural Networks, Random Forests, and Decision Trees.* This is with the aim of getting more information and advanced in mathematical and programming knowledge of the following concepts as discussed in this book:

- Tips of Theano in Logistic regression

- A model of code on how logistic regression code is written in Theano code

- MLP as a classifier in Logistic Regression

- In-depth into Neural Networks by looking into

✓ Convolutional Neural Networks

✓ Motivation

✓ Sparse connectivity

✓ Shared weights

- Mathematical explanation of the classes of learning algorithms like

- ✓ Linear methods

- ✓ Support vector machines

- ✓ Neural Networks

- ✓ Nearest Neighbor methods

- ● Classification of regression trees like

- ✓ Tree structured models

- ● Mathematical foundation of Random forests

- ✓ Bias variance decomposition

- ✓ Regression

- ● How random forests can be interpreted

- ✓ Decision trees

- ✓ Issues that are concerned with decision trees

Conclusion

Thank you for making it through to the end of *Machine Learning for Absolute Beginners: A Simple, Concise & Complete Introduction to Supervised and Unsupervised Learning Algorithms.* Let's hope that the book was informative enough and you were able to get all the tools that you need to achieve your goals whatever it is that they may be. Finishing this book does not mean that you have all the information to help you develop something concrete in this space.   You need to expand your horizons, and this will help you gain more experience and master you in the field of machine learning.

After reading this book, you will need to get practical from the theory that you have collected and brought change to the world through technological solutions to the challenges we face of processing information. There are companies that have come up with highly intelligent analytical systems that help organizations to analyze big data every day, to make business decisions. After reading this book, you now have a clue on how these complex systems come about, and you are on the forefront of being in a better place to create your system to process the kind of information you want.

Once you are done with the technical know-how on how supervised and unsupervised learning takes place, you will need to undergo a much more advanced study of the system, in order to formulate more complex systems. Finally, if you found this book useful in more than one way, a review on Amazon is much appreciated.